This Frayed Universe

poems by
Sarah Brashear

More books available from:

Etched Press
www.etchedpress.com

Also available in Amazon Kindle Store

First edition
Cover art "At Eternity's Gate" (1890) by Vincent van Gogh
Book design by Kevin Dublin

I dedicate this book to my encouraging family: my dad Daniel, my mother Linda, and my brothers Matt and Ethan. I also dedicate this book my wonderful, loving husband, Adam Brashear.

Acknowledgments

The author wishes to acknowledge the editors of the following publications in which a few of these poems first appeared in earlier forms:

Burning Word Press

Driftwood Press

Duende

Off The Coast Magazine

The Red Clay Review

Rufous City Review

Sediments

TABLE OF CONTENTS

How it Started

Later, in the foyer,
after the wine,
we talked about Aunt Margaret.
When she lost her eyes
she ran into the walls
and all I could do was laugh
as she fumbled
through the darkness.

We cut through pie,
but the pumpkin stuck to my throat.
I choked and from then on was afraid
of swallowing, chewing my food
to mush, if I ate at all.

My body was accustomed to the well-lit
cycles of the moon. It changed with them.

I let the bells toll, their dry, gray tongues
lap the earth's feet.

Now I'm caught in the slipstream.
I long for my summer body,
naked and cradled between
tunnels of fly-trap teeth and
volumes, volumes of lawn.

I bear witness to the ones who claim
the voices told them to jump.

Standing on this edge
I am an escape artist.

The Doctor Will See Me Now

In transit for a cold winter
I remember the stenciled speech patterns
of my father's figure
as it hovered over me serving breakfast
at 4 a.m. because neither of us could sleep.
His eyes were the great slants of the century,
his jaw rattled when he chewed.
He restored the tilt of my mind
back to balance.

My thoughts are muted, this bright
tear is the sound of its thawing.
I muddle through the slush,
It falls away like the rinsing of mud.

When I was six, I had a rash
convinced my skin was falling off.
Every day I hid my flakes in a drawer—this molting.

What's on the menu for today?
Psychotherapy, capsules, gels.
This comet tail of the off-world soars
into a haven, a place I can rest.

I Tell the Doctor I'm on Fire in My Dreams

I call it the white man curves
the way he looks as smoke rises behind him.
He tells me to live more pleasantly,
imitates God with his booming voice.
Asks me if the pills are working,
what I've been reading.
I watch him nod his head, scribble words
wait for demons to steam out of my body
with their grimy breaths.
My breathing convulses.
I tell him *I try to sleep but every time
I close my eyes I see that burning hand.*

Meth

Today, a miracle because no one vomits.
We eat grass like dogs, hunch on all fours
chase the white dragon until gel in the lava
lamp resembles our bodies.

The dinosaur language Vim chants when he's high
gives me tremors. Seismic waves crack my earth;
I cannot walk a straight line.

I swivel, grind my teeth,
lick Reynolds Wrap.

We sit in the patio, concentrate on bridged mountains:
their concrete necks, shelves that hold their rib cages.
The rock fragments, fingernails, jut from a sheet of skin.

My cheeks swell in the presence of his tongue.
I roll it around, remember how he tastes
in September, when his sinuses thicken
and the saliva in his mouth turns to syrup.

We cool down with water
that smells like last winter's snow.
We scribble letters on the breezeway floor
with crayons, try to write our names.

Holy Communion

We're closing in on God
you tell me, bite my lip
pull down my skirt,
skin wet as the day
I was born.

I have two loves this summer,
you and a bottle of Jack.

Flowers bud in your breath,
turn your cheeks a shade
of pink I've only ever seen in carnations.

I lie in the latitude of your language.
You keep me until night clogs our vision
the sun's gold brought to my fingertips.

The moon glitters around our eyes
we drop into laps and legs.
Light sends your body glistening
a tingle of seltzer.

I never looked as elegant as I do now,
Eucharist foaming in my throat.

A Word for Sadness

He says it's the trifecta: my body.
Marks my figure with highlighter trails
pauses at the wreaths around my thighs.

For years, I held my breath to save his oxygen,
walked slowly, pretended I was someone else
when all I wanted was to see through eyes, his hell.

I try to navigate detours,
Vim's hundred different words for sadness.
Tell me what the buildings offer,
he asks, waits for shingles to fall, a calculated distance.

I feel his vulgar rush of breath, this puddle he creates,
the light years we expand and bend
as we cross off the time it takes us,
in these huddled forms, to make love.

Catastrophe Day

Vim is a missile in the water, tears its skin
the blood doesn't have time to clot.
He swims at sundown every evening,
the red sun stirred in the sky with a stick.

He's of the broken blood vessel generation.
The mica shifts under my feet.

I only swim out to him when he's restless,
when his knees buckle and he collapses.

I knew it was a catastrophe day,
when, earlier, he slathered Crisco across his face
told me he was a mime.
The black bile in his mouth ran like battery acid.

The next morning I find him by the dock
tying the boat's rope to
his ankles. He announces: *If the anchor could hold*
The Great Medallion and keep it from sinking,
It should certainly save me.

This Frayed Universe

The day rises in installments.
I open my eyes to the fused film of fog.

When it breaks, I lift my window,
touchthesilltouchtheglasstouchthecurtain.

I wake in the absence of disaster
and fill my cup with bruises.

I'm allergic to air.
I tell Vim, as he hands me a hairbrush.

My hair is knotted again. I rake and unravel
the knots, suck on split ends.

I braid/unbraid.
Touchthestrandstouchthecombtouchhim.

I peel like sunburn,
a speck in this frayed universe.

My knees are cradle-capped. Rug burned and bare—
they slide against the carpet in my collapse.

I want to be his pollen in the mornings—
a patchwork piece of poetry,

but today I'm a torn cloth, a crater
in the center of his earth.

I stand, let the faucet rinse my chapped hands
and the sun squeeze like lotion through window.

Its rays dress me, and he watches
as the light dances along my hips.

The Kingdom Comes in Pieces

It started as a bet:
Thirty-five cents and some chewing gum.
I wouldn't lose my mind by February.

You lost,
my therapist tells me.

II

The pill bottle is empty in my pocket.

He asks me, *How many moons
did you swallow this time?*

III.

When the sinners call for me,
I'll be in the bedroom
with the sheets over my nocturnal face.

March Realization

I have found a vice grip
for this kind of sadness.

Today, the city melts.
The last drops of winter fall
as magnets that stick to the street.
The sun clears space in the sky.

We are crooked children,
falling bricks, broken flasks
our crispy consciences wheeled away
by barrows.

I hold onto the crust of a starling,
watch people walk
down this street
only to stand in solitude
and stare into colonies
of nature's skin.

I count gulls as they land
on our bodies against fleece
biting onto seeds
so that they can break through
the surface, shatter the (s)hell.

For our ailments, we are prescribed the world,
but all I remember is abandonment.

I Watch You on the Boardwalk

Every Saturday the traders come to sell.
I watch as you are pushed in your wagon, dead
feet hang off the side, two empty spigots.

You see things there, collect stamps
that fall on the wood panels,
lick the backs of them,
stick them to your stomach.
They hide under the loose wind of your shirt.

You don't speak. Just gaze at the close-up faces
of people selling T-shirts and hats,
photographs they'd taken, old rotary phones.

You were born into a land
that calls you by
your father's name:
cauliflower cheeks tuck behind
great stamen lashes
that magnify your face.
Your eyes tilt away.

The bridges of sky hold you up
but you're no child of dreams.
When you are handed a balloon,
you take it to your mouth
bite the red plastic 'til it shrivels,
dangles like licorice off your tongue.

Fever 102°

I am born from innocence.
A drip
     from violated sky.
This totem pole I head is growing tall.
I rise above air, a ticker tape parade.
Levitate through close towers
of distress calls and smoke signals.
This is what it's like to be a ghost.

I ride trolleys through the night, look inside
the windows of pubs and taverns.
Shapes of faces become blurs of color.
I think they smile,
but the wind laughs at my indecency.

These flames only throw
when I'm fire-engine red
with a degree of calamity.
The spike of breathing
is a mountain peak. Tomorrow
I hope to level out,
indulge in the tantric afterglow
of an honorary high.
The cauldron of night leaks into day.
With strips of my body gone,
small seconds left in the universe.

Zion Lutheran Church

Everything you hold in the Bible
of your brain shakes static.

You speak to the boilers.
Goblins in the walls hover beside your bed,
Dark marks in the fire are liver spots,
rest on skin, a lumped toad.

You forget to turn off the burner
after you light your cigarette—
Can no longer remember which state
the Yankees play for,
the name of the church
where you were married,

but you remember God.
You hear Him hang above you.
He is a bat. You listen
to the Gloria Patri, try to sing along,
sit on your stairs and rub cream
across your chest instead
of your face, turn off the lamp
instead of the tap.

Mad Boy Stirs

The morning they take him he
is eating a flower.
The pollen leaves yellow stains
around his lips. He looks like a clown.
Smiling, he grabs fistfuls of grass
to keep himself balanced.

He claws with wild eyes,
refuses the earth's medicines
of orange lava drops and pesticides.
Not a whole person but
a quarantined half.
The bell rings for supper, he comes.
The light flickers in the hall. The small peel
stretches over him, a silkworm.
He slips across the soft feather of floor
that holds him upright.

The red hot strips of winter burn his feet.
He's walking on ice,
too dark to be full of day.
Electric blue pills, belly up
clink in his hands, ice crystals.

He's a Golden Chain Tree, his branches grow,
grow out of me, arms flake, limbs flail.
To be the sweat that sticks to him,
bark that spills from him,
black cherry smoke that spins in sea sick circles,
as his eyes shut to the world.

Every morning he jumps over torches
and midday he is caught by candlelight.
He burns   he burns   he burns.

Let's Pretend the Mountains
Are Our Husbands

she whispers, claims the peak
with the most snow, says it will keep
her warm, a deer hide. I pose
and curtsey to the land, skim the tops
of the Appalachians—their heavy chests
piles of rock, sturdy. The birds
give me energy: I watch as they circle.
I stretch out my hands like I'm flying.
Stand tall in the open field, to prove
I am vertical.

Here, In the Realm of Everything

The second time I fall out of the sky
it's an accident.
My body tumbles through a crest.

Heavy, I drop at his feet.
He half-holds me like a bag of apples,
I drip winesap, gala.

He examines me, finds my rough spots,
brown holes where worms chewed through,
left me softened.

Now I rely on air to fill crevices in my body.

A storm approaches.
I'm reminded of the stove's open eye
as dad lit a cigarette from the burner
because I hid all the lighters.

I want him to know this:
If I could find a way to escape
this whale-belly world, I would.